MW01133447

Justice

Amanda Rondeau

Consulting Editor
Monica Marx, M.A./Reading Specialist

Published by SandCastle™, an imprint of ABDO Publishing Company, 4940 Viking Drive, Edina, Minnesota 55435.

Printed in the United States.

Credits
Edited by: Pam Price
Curriculum Coordinator: Nancy Tuminelly
Cover and Interior Design and Production: Mighty Media
Photo Credits: Corbis Images, Eyewire Images, PhotoDisc

Library of Congress Cataloging-in-Publication Data
Rondeau, Amanda, 1974-
    Justice / Amanda Rondeau.
       p. cm. -- (United we stand)
    Includes index.
    Summary: Defines justice as fair and impartial behavior or treatment and cites such examples as the enforcement of laws in a country, equal treatment of everyone in a classroom, and the maintenance of rules in the home.
    ISBN 1-57765-879-5
    1. Justice--Juvenile literature. [1. Justice. 2. Fairness.] I. Title. II. Series.

JC578 .R65 2002
340'.11--dc21

                                                                    2002066403

SandCastle™ books are created by a professional team of educators, reading specialists, and content developers around five essential components that include phonemic awareness, phonics, vocabulary, text comprehension, and fluency. All books are written, reviewed, and leveled for guided reading, early intervention reading, and Accelerated Reader® programs and designed for use in shared, guided, and independent reading and writing activities to support a balanced approach to literacy instruction.

Let Us Know

After reading the book, SandCastle would like you to tell us your stories about reading. What is your favorite page? Was there something hard that you needed help with? Share the ups and downs of learning to read. We want to hear from you! To get posted on the ABDO Publishing Company Web site, send us email at:

sandcastle@abdopub.com

SandCastle Level: Transitional

What is justice?

Justice means treating everyone the same no matter who they are.

People vote in elections to decide who our leaders will be.

Some of these leaders help make our laws.

Laws are part of the justice system.

Laws help us treat everyone fairly.

The people in the justice system help make sure our laws are fair.

It is the job of the police to enforce the laws and provide safety.

They are part of the justice system.

Sometimes people need help to make sure they are treated fairly.

We have judges and lawyers who help them.

Judges and lawyers are part of the justice system.

There are other types of justice.

My teacher treats everyone the same.

She is a fair teacher.

We have rules at home.

The rules are the same for my sister and me.

Our mom treats us fairly.

We follow rules when we play.

Then we know we are being fair.

Who do you know that is part of the justice system?

(the police)

Index

Glossary

enforce   to make sure laws and rules are followed

judge   a person who listens to court cases and decides on punishment for a guilty person

justice   treating everyone fairly

laws   rules that are set by the government

lawyer   a person whose job it is to know the law and to speak for people in court

rule   an established regulation that tells you what you must or must not do

About SandCastle™

A professional team of educators, reading specialists, and content developers created the SandCastle™ series to support young readers as they develop reading skills and strategies and increase their general knowledge. The SandCastle™ series has four levels that correspond to early literacy development in young children. The levels are provided to help teachers and parents select the appropriate books for young readers.

Emerging Readers
(no flags)

Beginning Readers
(1 flag)

Transitional Readers
(2 flags)

Fluent Readers
(3 flags)

These levels are meant only as a guide. All levels are subject to change.

To see a complete list of SandCastle™ books and other nonfiction titles from ABDO Publishing Company, visit **www.abdopub.com** or contact us at:

4940 Viking Drive, Edina, Minnesota 55435 • 1-800-800-1312 • fax: 1-952-831-1632